My Life TRACKER

A HABIT JOURNAL TO HELP YOU MAP OUT AND MANAGE YOUR LIFE

ANNA BARNES

MY LIFE TRACKER

Text by Sarah Butterworth

An Hachette UK Company
www.hachette.co.uk

Vie Books, an imprint of Summersdale Publishers Ltd
Part of Octopus Publishing Group Limited
Carmelite House
50 Victoria Embankment
LONDON
EC4Y 0DZ
UK

www.summersdale.com

Printed and bound in China

ISBN: 978-1-80007-447-7

Substantial discounts on bulk quantities of Summersdale books are available to corporations, professional associations and other organizations. For details contact general enquiries: telephone: +44 (0) 1243 771107 or email: enquiries@summersdale.com.

Disclaimer

This book is not intended as a substitute for the medical advice of a doctor or physician. If you are experiencing problems with your health, it is always best to follow the advice of a medical professional.

Introduction

"How's life?"

"Fine."

This book is for people who want more than fine, who want to live life to the full, rather than letting the days, months or years float by in the busyness of day-to-day existence.

Everything we do is interconnected, so it's good to understand life as a whole: how does my social media use affect my sleep? How does my sleep pattern affect my mood? How does my mood affect the spending decisions I make? And so on. Those who take a "big picture" approach to their lives are better able to cope with challenges and overwhelming situations, and thus they are both more relaxed and more successful.

By tracking different elements of your life, you will be able to step back, like a kingfisher gently hovering over the water, surveying the whole scene, knowing exactly where to strike. You will be able to see

what's working well and what's holding you back; you will become more self-aware and empowered to make small changes that make a big difference.

Packed into this small but mighty book are all the tools you need to keep track of your spending, your health, your mood and more. Broken down by month and day, these trackers are easy and fun to use. All you need are a few minutes each day and some colouring pencils; think of this book as your daily check-in with yourself. You'll also find words of wisdom and encouragement as well as helpful hints and tips. After a few months you may see patterns emerge, or you may spot habits that are affecting other areas of your life. This book aims to help you discover what you need to do in order to make the tweaks necessary to live your best life.

January

MY GOALS AND ACHIEVEMENTS

My goal(s) for this month:

Example goal: Spend ten minutes in quiet at the start of every weekday

What will I do to reach my goal(s)?

Example steps: Start with every other day, set an early morning alarm, find a space free of distractions, let the other members of my household know and ask them not to disturb me

Top Tips

MAKE RESOLUTIONS STICK

Studies suggest that 80 per cent of New Year's resolutions fail. This is because people often make big plans to change their behaviour without considering their habits and attitudes.

Setting goals is good, but writing them down or sharing them with a friend is even better because you can check in with your progress and feel more motivated. Another way to encourage success is to make your goal achievable; it's better to consider a long-term aim and then break it down into small manageable steps that you can work toward each month. This way you will be more likely to achieve your January goal and this in turn will encourage and motivate you to achieve your February goal. Don't be discouraged if you fail one day – simply use your tracker to help you understand what habits might be getting in your way.

Spending Tracker

SURVIVAL		CULTURE	
Food shop	42.35	Cinema	11.95

SURVIVAL: Regular, necessary expenditure, such as food, childcare or transport.

CULTURE: Expenditure on cultural activities, theatre, books, etc.

Total income per month: _____

Income minus fixed costs: _____

OPTIONAL		EXTRA	
Dinner Out	23.27	B-day card	2.50

OPTIONAL: Anything you choose to spend money on, like a social event or meal out.

EXTRA: Anything irregular or unexpected, such as repairs or birthday presents.

Water Tracker

One drop = one glass (400 ml)

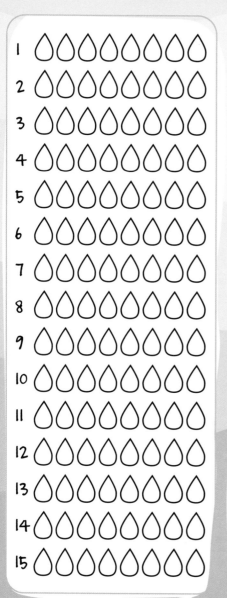

Sleep Tracker

KEY

- ◯ Four hours or fewer
- ◯ Five hours
- ◯ Six hours
- ◯ Seven hours
- ◯ Eight hours
- ◯ Nine hours or more

Exercise Tracker

Use this page to log your activity levels this month.
Write in the number of active minutes for each day
or colour-code each box.

1	2	3	4
5	6	7	8
9	10	11	12
13	14	15	16
17	18	19	20
21	22	23	24
25	26	27	28
29	30	31	

Active
Moderate
Rest

Mindfulness Tracker

If you had a moment of mindfulness today, record it here by colouring in the spiral.

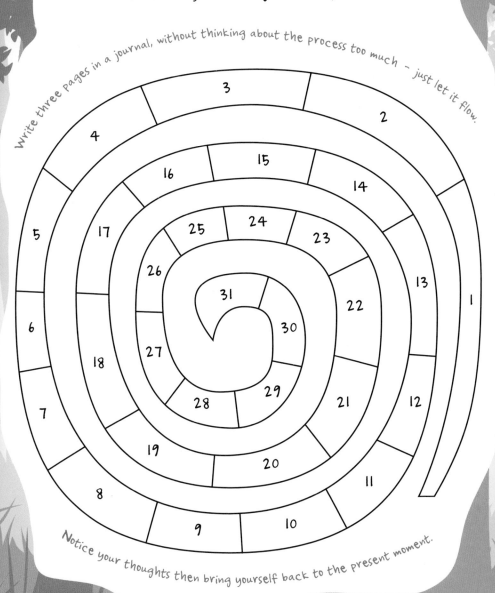

Write three pages in a journal, without thinking about the process too much – just let it flow.

Notice your thoughts then bring yourself back to the present moment.

Mood Tracker

Great   Good   Average   Poor   Terrible

Social Media Tracker

One heart = 30 minutes

1 ♡♡♡♡♡♡♡
2 ♡♡♡♡♡♡♡
3 ♡♡♡♡♡♡♡
4 ♡♡♡♡♡♡♡
5 ♡♡♡♡♡♡♡
6 ♡♡♡♡♡♡♡
7 ♡♡♡♡♡♡♡
8 ♡♡♡♡♡♡♡
9 ♡♡♡♡♡♡♡
10 ♡♡♡♡♡♡♡
11 ♡♡♡♡♡♡♡
12 ♡♡♡♡♡♡♡
13 ♡♡♡♡♡♡♡
14 ♡♡♡♡♡♡♡
15 ♡♡♡♡♡♡♡

16 ♡♡♡♡♡♡♡
17 ♡♡♡♡♡♡♡
18 ♡♡♡♡♡♡♡
19 ♡♡♡♡♡♡♡
20 ♡♡♡♡♡♡♡
21 ♡♡♡♡♡♡♡
22 ♡♡♡♡♡♡♡
23 ♡♡♡♡♡♡♡
24 ♡♡♡♡♡♡♡
25 ♡♡♡♡♡♡♡
26 ♡♡♡♡♡♡♡
27 ♡♡♡♡♡♡♡
28 ♡♡♡♡♡♡♡
29 ♡♡♡♡♡♡♡
30 ♡♡♡♡♡♡♡
31 ♡♡♡♡♡♡♡

Media Tracker

Use this page to track the books you've read
and the TV shows and films you've watched
this month and your rating out of five.

Books read this month:

_____ ☆☆☆☆☆

_____ ☆☆☆☆☆

_____ ☆☆☆☆☆

_____ ☆☆☆☆☆

_____ ☆☆☆☆☆

_____ ☆☆☆☆☆

Films and TV shows watched this month:

_____ ☆☆☆☆☆

_____ ☆☆☆☆☆

_____ ☆☆☆☆☆

_____ ☆☆☆☆☆

_____ ☆☆☆☆☆

_____ ☆☆☆☆☆

A journey of a
thousand miles
begins with a
single step.

LAO TZU

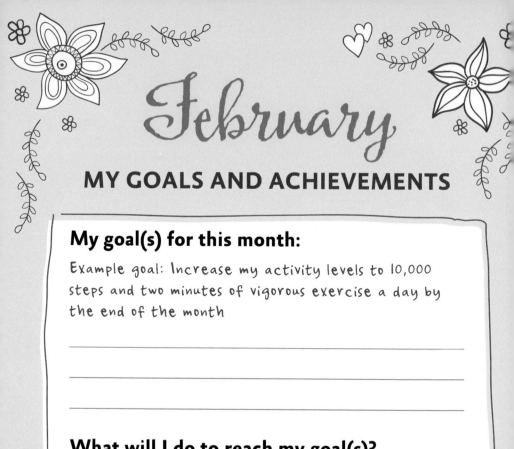

February

MY GOALS AND ACHIEVEMENTS

My goal(s) for this month:

Example goal: Increase my activity levels to 10,000 steps and two minutes of vigorous exercise a day by the end of the month

_____

_____

_____

What will I do to reach my goal(s)?

Example steps: Go for a walk at least once a day, aim to get to 10,000 steps a day, start jogging for two minutes during daily walk

_____

_____

_____

Top Tips

KEEP YOUR SPIRITS UP

The rest of us can learn a lot from the Scandinavian countries. While many of us complain about the humdrum aspects of everyday life, the Danes find joy in simple living and even have a word for it: *hygge*. *Hygge* is associated with feelings of comfort, contentment and cosiness. Great to focus on any time of year, try these things to make your life more *hygge*.

- Eat well: Enjoy the comfort and nutrition of winter stews and soups or crisp summer salads.

- Get outside: Whether it's a long, shaded stomp around the woods, a wet and muddy run in the rain or a simple five-minute stroll in the park, enjoy the feeling of fresh air filling your lungs. If it's cold, snuggle up with a hot drink and a cosy blanket when you get in. Bliss.

- Start a gratitude diary: Even on a bad day you can find something to be grateful for. Focusing on the positive helps us to feel happier both short and long term.

- Spend time with the people you love: It'll give you an instant boost of happiness.

- Practise self-compassion: Be kind, gentle and positive with yourself. Treat yourself to occasional indulgences and make time to do the things you enjoy.

Spending Tracker

MONTH: FEBRUARY

SURVIVAL		CULTURE	
Food shop	42.35	Cinema	11.95

SURVIVAL: Regular, necessary expenditure, such as food, childcare or transport.

CULTURE: Expenditure on cultural activities, theatre, books, etc.

Total income per month: _____

Income minus fixed costs: _____

OPTIONAL		EXTRA	
Dinner Out	23.27	B-day card	2.50

OPTIONAL: Anything you choose to spend money on, like a social event or meal out.

EXTRA: Anything irregular or unexpected, such as repairs or birthday presents.

Water Tracker

One drop = one glass (400 ml)

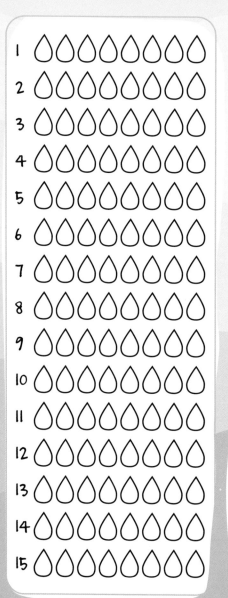

1 ⬦⬦⬦⬦⬦⬦⬦
2 ⬦⬦⬦⬦⬦⬦⬦
3 ⬦⬦⬦⬦⬦⬦⬦
4 ⬦⬦⬦⬦⬦⬦⬦
5 ⬦⬦⬦⬦⬦⬦⬦
6 ⬦⬦⬦⬦⬦⬦⬦
7 ⬦⬦⬦⬦⬦⬦⬦
8 ⬦⬦⬦⬦⬦⬦⬦
9 ⬦⬦⬦⬦⬦⬦⬦
10 ⬦⬦⬦⬦⬦⬦⬦
11 ⬦⬦⬦⬦⬦⬦⬦
12 ⬦⬦⬦⬦⬦⬦⬦
13 ⬦⬦⬦⬦⬦⬦⬦
14 ⬦⬦⬦⬦⬦⬦⬦
15 ⬦⬦⬦⬦⬦⬦⬦

16 ⬦⬦⬦⬦⬦⬦⬦
17 ⬦⬦⬦⬦⬦⬦⬦
18 ⬦⬦⬦⬦⬦⬦⬦
19 ⬦⬦⬦⬦⬦⬦⬦
20 ⬦⬦⬦⬦⬦⬦⬦
21 ⬦⬦⬦⬦⬦⬦⬦
22 ⬦⬦⬦⬦⬦⬦⬦
23 ⬦⬦⬦⬦⬦⬦⬦
24 ⬦⬦⬦⬦⬦⬦⬦
25 ⬦⬦⬦⬦⬦⬦⬦
26 ⬦⬦⬦⬦⬦⬦⬦
27 ⬦⬦⬦⬦⬦⬦⬦
28 ⬦⬦⬦⬦⬦⬦⬦
29 ⬦⬦⬦⬦⬦⬦⬦

Sleep Tracker

KEY

- ◯ Four hours or fewer
- ◯ Five hours
- ◯ Six hours
- ◯ Seven hours
- ◯ Eight hours
- ◯ Nine hours or more

Exercise Tracker

Use this page to log your activity levels this month.
Write in the number of active minutes for each day
or colour-code each box.

1	2	3	4
5	6	7	8
9	10	11	12
13	14	15	16
17	18	19	20
21	22	23	24
25	26	27	28

29

○ Active
○ Moderate
○ Rest

Mindfulness Tracker

If you had a moment of mindfulness today, record it here by colouring in the spiral.

Write a list of things that make you smile.

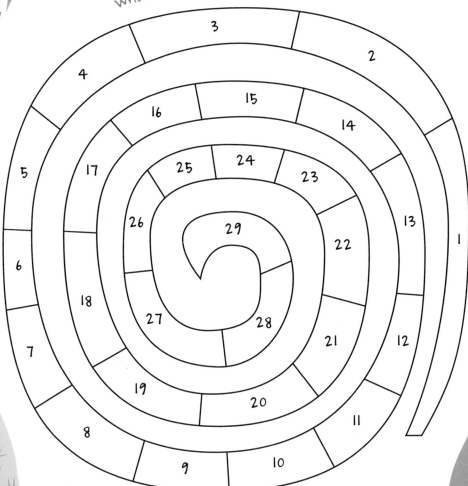

Meditate on a happy memory, trying to remember the sensations you felt at that time.

Mood Tracker

Great   Good   Average   Poor   Terrible

Social Media Tracker

One heart = 30 minutes

1 ♡♡♡♡♡♡♡
2 ♡♡♡♡♡♡♡
3 ♡♡♡♡♡♡♡
4 ♡♡♡♡♡♡♡
5 ♡♡♡♡♡♡♡
6 ♡♡♡♡♡♡♡
7 ♡♡♡♡♡♡♡
8 ♡♡♡♡♡♡♡
9 ♡♡♡♡♡♡♡
10 ♡♡♡♡♡♡♡
11 ♡♡♡♡♡♡♡
12 ♡♡♡♡♡♡♡
13 ♡♡♡♡♡♡♡
14 ♡♡♡♡♡♡♡
15 ♡♡♡♡♡♡♡

16 ♡♡♡♡♡♡♡
17 ♡♡♡♡♡♡♡
18 ♡♡♡♡♡♡♡
19 ♡♡♡♡♡♡♡
20 ♡♡♡♡♡♡♡
21 ♡♡♡♡♡♡♡
22 ♡♡♡♡♡♡♡
23 ♡♡♡♡♡♡♡
24 ♡♡♡♡♡♡♡
25 ♡♡♡♡♡♡♡
26 ♡♡♡♡♡♡♡
27 ♡♡♡♡♡♡♡
28 ♡♡♡♡♡♡♡
29 ♡♡♡♡♡♡♡

Media Tracker

Use this page to track the books you've read
and the TV shows and films you've watched
this month and your rating out of five.

Books read this month:

Films and TV shows watched this month:

KEEP MOVING FORWARD
ONE STEP AT A TIME

March

MY GOALS AND ACHIEVEMENTS

My goal(s) for this month:

Example goal: Find a form of exercise I enjoy

_____

_____

_____

What will I do to reach my goal(s)?

Example steps: Take a trial gym membership;
try out the different classes, join in with friend's
exercise routines and try the things they enjoy,
build the exercise I enjoy into my routine

_____

_____

_____

_____

Top Tips

MAKE EXERCISE FUN

You've got new trainers, downloaded an app, and psyched yourself up: you're taking up running. Rain is bouncing off the ground, it's freezing, and you start to feel a little sick.

With memories of dreaded laps of the school track in the back of your mind, you force yourself round the park, imagining your scary teacher shouting at you to run faster. You hate every minute of it, but you are determined to get fit so you're going to keep it up. You manage two weeks.

Exercise isn't supposed to be a punishment – if you dread doing it, you're more likely to give it up. If you know you've always hated something, and you know you're going to go through hell to do it, then don't. Do something you love. As a child, did you hate running but love riding your bike? Take up cycling instead. Not the sporty type? Then think outside the box; join a tango class and learn to dance, take up martial arts and learn self-defence, buy a skateboard or a pair of roller skates and hit your local skate park. Whatever you do, have fun. You're more likely to keep it up if you enjoy it.

Spending Tracker

SURVIVAL		CULTURE	
Food shop	42.35	Cinema	11.95

SURVIVAL: Regular, necessary expenditure, such as food, childcare or transport.

CULTURE: Expenditure on cultural activities, theatre, books, etc.

Total income per month: _____

Income minus fixed costs:_____

OPTIONAL		EXTRA	
Dinner Out	23.27	B-day card	2.50

OPTIONAL: Anything you choose to spend money on, like a social event or meal out.

EXTRA: Anything irregular or unexpected, such as repairs or birthday presents.

Water Tracker

One drop = one glass (400 ml)

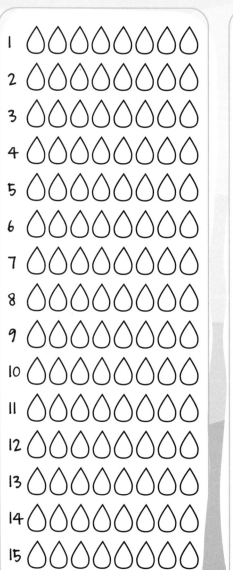

1 ○○○○○○○
2 ○○○○○○○
3 ○○○○○○○
4 ○○○○○○○
5 ○○○○○○○
6 ○○○○○○○
7 ○○○○○○○
8 ○○○○○○○
9 ○○○○○○○
10 ○○○○○○○
11 ○○○○○○○
12 ○○○○○○○
13 ○○○○○○○
14 ○○○○○○○
15 ○○○○○○○

16 ○○○○○○○
17 ○○○○○○○
18 ○○○○○○○
19 ○○○○○○○
20 ○○○○○○○
21 ○○○○○○○
22 ○○○○○○○
23 ○○○○○○○
24 ○○○○○○○
25 ○○○○○○○
26 ○○○○○○○
27 ○○○○○○○
28 ○○○○○○○
29 ○○○○○○○
30 ○○○○○○○
31 ○○○○○○○

Sleep Tracker

KEY

- ☐ Four hours or fewer
- ☐ Five hours
- ☐ Six hours
- ☐ Seven hours
- ☐ Eight hours
- ☐ Nine hours or more

Exercise Tracker

Use this page to log your activity levels this month.
Write in the number of active minutes for each day
or colour-code each box.

1	2	3	4
5	6	7	8
9	10	11	12
13	14	15	16
17	18	19	20
21	22	23	24
25	26	27	28
29	30	31	

○ Active
○ Moderate
○ Rest

Mindfulness Tracker

If you had a moment of mindfulness today, record it here by colouring in the spiral.

Close your eyes and scan your body, focusing on each part in turn. What sensations do you notice?

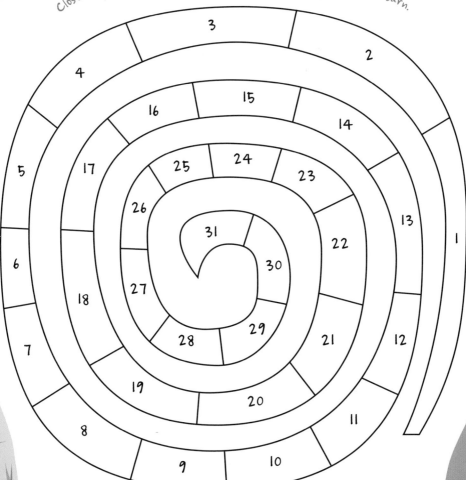

Remind yourself that emotions are never permanent.

Mood Tracker

Great   Good   Average   Poor   Terrible

Social Media Tracker

One heart = 30 minutes

1 ♡♡♡♡♡♡♡
2 ♡♡♡♡♡♡♡
3 ♡♡♡♡♡♡♡
4 ♡♡♡♡♡♡♡
5 ♡♡♡♡♡♡♡
6 ♡♡♡♡♡♡♡
7 ♡♡♡♡♡♡♡
8 ♡♡♡♡♡♡♡
9 ♡♡♡♡♡♡♡
10 ♡♡♡♡♡♡♡
11 ♡♡♡♡♡♡♡
12 ♡♡♡♡♡♡♡
13 ♡♡♡♡♡♡♡
14 ♡♡♡♡♡♡♡
15 ♡♡♡♡♡♡♡

16 ♡♡♡♡♡♡♡
17 ♡♡♡♡♡♡♡
18 ♡♡♡♡♡♡♡
19 ♡♡♡♡♡♡♡
20 ♡♡♡♡♡♡♡
21 ♡♡♡♡♡♡♡
22 ♡♡♡♡♡♡♡
23 ♡♡♡♡♡♡♡
24 ♡♡♡♡♡♡♡
25 ♡♡♡♡♡♡♡
26 ♡♡♡♡♡♡♡
27 ♡♡♡♡♡♡♡
28 ♡♡♡♡♡♡♡
29 ♡♡♡♡♡♡♡
30 ♡♡♡♡♡♡♡
31 ♡♡♡♡♡♡♡

Media Tracker

Use this page to track the books you've read and the TV shows and films you've watched this month and your rating out of five.

Books read this month:

_____ ☆☆☆☆☆
_____ ☆☆☆☆☆
_____ ☆☆☆☆☆
_____ ☆☆☆☆☆
_____ ☆☆☆☆☆
_____ ☆☆☆☆☆

Films and TV shows watched this month:

_____ ☆☆☆☆☆
_____ ☆☆☆☆☆
_____ ☆☆☆☆☆
_____ ☆☆☆☆☆
_____ ☆☆☆☆☆
_____ ☆☆☆☆☆

Do what you love;
you'll be better at it.
It sounds pretty simple,
but you'd be surprised
how many people don't
get this one right away.

LL COOL J

April

MY GOALS AND ACHIEVEMENTS

My goal(s) for this month:

Example goal: Spend time outside every day

_____

_____

_____

What will I do to reach my goal(s)?

Example steps: Check the weather forecast each day to be prepared, take a packed lunch to the park on my lunch break on sunny days, plan a trip out with friends two weekends of the month

_____

_____

_____

_____

Top Tips

WHY THE GREAT OUTDOORS IS GREAT

There's nothing quite like the great outdoors for nourishing the soul. Being outdoors not only gives us an opportunity for exercise, it provides us with vitamin D and boosts our immune system. It also gives us a break from the hustle and bustle of our busy lives and can create a wonderful sense of inner peace. A bit of time spent in the countryside, on the beach or in the local park can increase our problem-solving skills and boost our creativity by up to 50 per cent. So, switch off the TV, close the laptop, put the phone on silent and head into the wilds (or maybe just the back garden).

You might fancy a long hike or a camping trip (don't forget the campfire and the marshmallows!). But if adventure isn't your thing, sitting in the garden with a book or on a park bench watching the world go by can provide those much-needed moments of solitude and calm in the hubbub of a busy week.

Spending Tracker

SURVIVAL		CULTURE	
Food shop	42.35	Cinema	11.95

SURVIVAL: Regular, necessary expenditure, such as food, childcare or transport.

CULTURE: Expenditure on cultural activities, theatre, books, etc.

Total income per month: _____

Income minus fixed costs: _____

OPTIONAL		EXTRA	
Dinner Out	23.27	B-day card	2.50

OPTIONAL: Anything you choose to spend money on, like a social event or meal out.

EXTRA: Anything irregular or unexpected, such as repairs or birthday presents.

Water Tracker

One drop = one glass (400 ml)

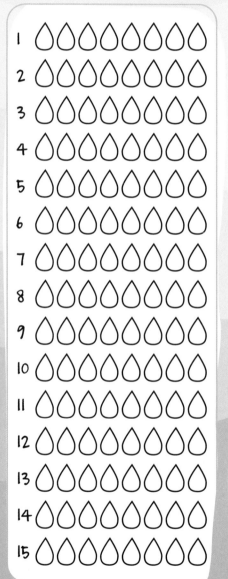

1 ⬦⬦⬦⬦⬦⬦⬦⬦	16 ⬦⬦⬦⬦⬦⬦⬦⬦
2 ⬦⬦⬦⬦⬦⬦⬦⬦	17 ⬦⬦⬦⬦⬦⬦⬦⬦
3 ⬦⬦⬦⬦⬦⬦⬦⬦	18 ⬦⬦⬦⬦⬦⬦⬦⬦
4 ⬦⬦⬦⬦⬦⬦⬦⬦	19 ⬦⬦⬦⬦⬦⬦⬦⬦
5 ⬦⬦⬦⬦⬦⬦⬦⬦	20 ⬦⬦⬦⬦⬦⬦⬦⬦
6 ⬦⬦⬦⬦⬦⬦⬦⬦	21 ⬦⬦⬦⬦⬦⬦⬦⬦
7 ⬦⬦⬦⬦⬦⬦⬦⬦	22 ⬦⬦⬦⬦⬦⬦⬦⬦
8 ⬦⬦⬦⬦⬦⬦⬦⬦	23 ⬦⬦⬦⬦⬦⬦⬦⬦
9 ⬦⬦⬦⬦⬦⬦⬦⬦	24 ⬦⬦⬦⬦⬦⬦⬦⬦
10 ⬦⬦⬦⬦⬦⬦⬦⬦	25 ⬦⬦⬦⬦⬦⬦⬦⬦
11 ⬦⬦⬦⬦⬦⬦⬦⬦	26 ⬦⬦⬦⬦⬦⬦⬦⬦
12 ⬦⬦⬦⬦⬦⬦⬦⬦	27 ⬦⬦⬦⬦⬦⬦⬦⬦
13 ⬦⬦⬦⬦⬦⬦⬦⬦	28 ⬦⬦⬦⬦⬦⬦⬦⬦
14 ⬦⬦⬦⬦⬦⬦⬦⬦	29 ⬦⬦⬦⬦⬦⬦⬦⬦
15 ⬦⬦⬦⬦⬦⬦⬦⬦	30 ⬦⬦⬦⬦⬦⬦⬦⬦

Sleep Tracker

KEY

- [ ] Four hours or fewer
- [ ] Five hours
- [ ] Six hours
- [ ] Seven hours
- [ ] Eight hours
- [ ] Nine hours or more

Exercise Tracker

Use this page to log your activity levels this month.
Write in the number of active minutes for each day
or colour-code each box.

1	2	3	4
5	6	7	8
9	10	11	12
13	14	15	16
17	18	19	20
21	22	23	24
25	26	27	28
29	30		

○ Active
○ Moderate
○ Rest

Mindfulness Tracker

If you had a moment of mindfulness today, record it here by colouring in the spiral.

Take a walk and observe the sights, sounds and smells around you.

3

4

2

15

16

14

5

17

25

24

23

26

30

13

22

1

6

18

27

29

7

28

21

12

19

20

11

8

9

10

When walking, take notice of each step
and how you connect with the ground beneath you.

Mood Tracker

Great Good Average Poor Terrible

Social Media Tracker

One heart = 30 minutes

1 ♡♡♡♡♡♡♡
2 ♡♡♡♡♡♡♡
3 ♡♡♡♡♡♡♡
4 ♡♡♡♡♡♡♡
5 ♡♡♡♡♡♡♡
6 ♡♡♡♡♡♡♡
7 ♡♡♡♡♡♡♡
8 ♡♡♡♡♡♡♡
9 ♡♡♡♡♡♡♡
10 ♡♡♡♡♡♡♡
11 ♡♡♡♡♡♡♡
12 ♡♡♡♡♡♡♡
13 ♡♡♡♡♡♡♡
14 ♡♡♡♡♡♡♡
15 ♡♡♡♡♡♡♡

16 ♡♡♡♡♡♡♡
17 ♡♡♡♡♡♡♡
18 ♡♡♡♡♡♡♡
19 ♡♡♡♡♡♡♡
20 ♡♡♡♡♡♡♡
21 ♡♡♡♡♡♡♡
22 ♡♡♡♡♡♡♡
23 ♡♡♡♡♡♡♡
24 ♡♡♡♡♡♡♡
25 ♡♡♡♡♡♡♡
26 ♡♡♡♡♡♡♡
27 ♡♡♡♡♡♡♡
28 ♡♡♡♡♡♡♡
29 ♡♡♡♡♡♡♡
30 ♡♡♡♡♡♡♡

Media Tracker

Use this page to track the books you've read
and the TV shows and films you've watched
this month and your rating out of five.

Books read this month:

_____ ☆☆☆☆☆

_____ ☆☆☆☆☆

_____ ☆☆☆☆☆

_____ ☆☆☆☆☆

_____ ☆☆☆☆☆

_____ ☆☆☆☆☆

Films and TV shows watched this month:

_____ ☆☆☆☆☆

_____ ☆☆☆☆☆

_____ ☆☆☆☆☆

_____ ☆☆☆☆☆

_____ ☆☆☆☆☆

_____ ☆☆☆☆☆

SOMETIMES IT'S
GOOD TO JUST STOP
AND BREATHE —
FEEL THE MOMENT

May

MY GOALS AND ACHIEVEMENTS

My goal(s) for this month:

Example goal: Join a club and develop a hobby that I enjoy

_____

_____

_____

What will I do to reach my goal(s)?

Example steps: Research local clubs of my chosen hobby, send an email asking about joining, be brave, take a deep breath and remind myself that it's good to do new things

_____

_____

_____

_____

Top Tips

PRIORITIZE FOR SUCCESS

Sometimes we're so busy with work and life admin that we don't manage to make time to do the things that we really value. Being constantly busy but not achieving the things you want to can be demoralizing.

Think of those precious 24 hours as your daily "budget" to spend. Just like you would with money, aim to strike a healthy balance between what you want and what you need. Look for ways to reduce "spending" on the necessary aspects of life, such as chores (do you really need to iron everything?) so that you have more left over for tasks that are either important or fun. And, just as you accept that sometimes you can't *have* it all, accept that you might not be able to always *do* it all either.

Balance is key, so aim to fit rest, fun, exercise and productivity into your schedule in equal measures.

Spending Tracker

MONTH: MAY

SURVIVAL		CULTURE	
Food shop	42.35	Cinema	11.95

SURVIVAL: Regular, necessary expenditure, such as food, childcare or transport.

CULTURE: Expenditure on cultural activities, theatre, books, etc.

Total income per month: _____

Income minus fixed costs:_____

OPTIONAL		EXTRA	
Dinner Out	23.27	B-day card	2.50

OPTIONAL: Anything you choose to spend money on, like a social event or meal out.

EXTRA: Anything irregular or unexpected, such as repairs or birthday presents.

Water Tracker

One drop = one glass (400 ml)

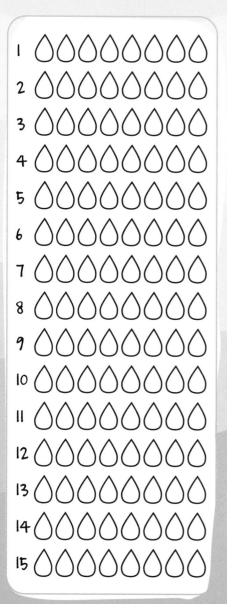

1 ○○○○○○○○
2 ○○○○○○○○
3 ○○○○○○○○
4 ○○○○○○○○
5 ○○○○○○○○
6 ○○○○○○○○
7 ○○○○○○○○
8 ○○○○○○○○
9 ○○○○○○○○
10 ○○○○○○○○
11 ○○○○○○○○
12 ○○○○○○○○
13 ○○○○○○○○
14 ○○○○○○○○
15 ○○○○○○○○

16 ○○○○○○○○
17 ○○○○○○○○
18 ○○○○○○○○
19 ○○○○○○○○
20 ○○○○○○○○
21 ○○○○○○○○
22 ○○○○○○○○
23 ○○○○○○○○
24 ○○○○○○○○
25 ○○○○○○○○
26 ○○○○○○○○
27 ○○○○○○○○
28 ○○○○○○○○
29 ○○○○○○○○
30 ○○○○○○○○
31 ○○○○○○○○

Sleep Tracker

KEY

- ⬜ Four hours or fewer
- ⬜ Five hours
- ⬜ Six hours
- ⬜ Seven hours
- ⬜ Eight hours
- ⬜ Nine hours or more

Exercise Tracker

Use this page to log your activity levels this month. Write in the number of active minutes for each day or colour-code each box.

1	2	3	4
5	6	7	8
9	10	11	12
13	14	15	16
17	18	19	20
21	22	23	24
25	26	27	28
29	30	31	

◯ Active
◯ Moderate
◯ Rest

Mindfulness Tracker

If you had a moment of mindfulness today, record it here by colouring in the spiral.

Focus on one task at a time.

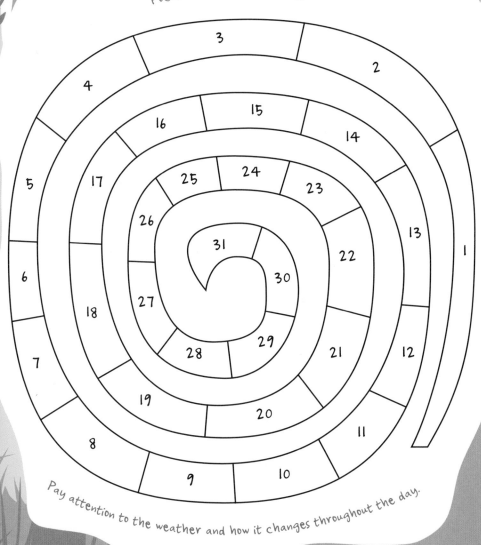

Pay attention to the weather and how it changes throughout the day.

Mood Tracker

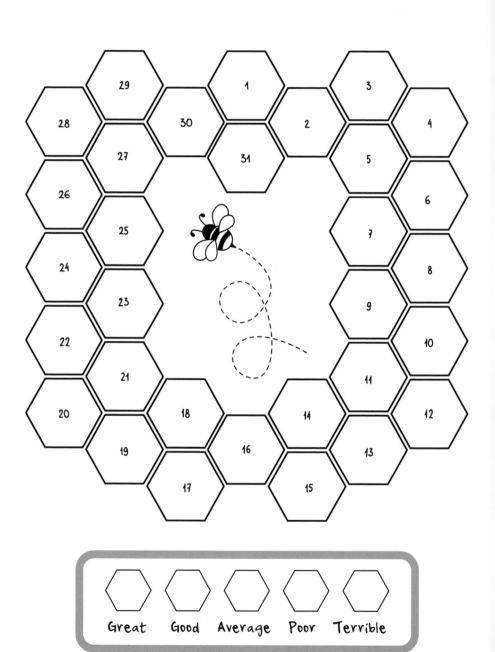

Great   Good   Average   Poor   Terrible

Social Media Tracker

One heart = 30 minutes

1 ♡♡♡♡♡♡♡
2 ♡♡♡♡♡♡♡
3 ♡♡♡♡♡♡♡
4 ♡♡♡♡♡♡♡
5 ♡♡♡♡♡♡♡
6 ♡♡♡♡♡♡♡
7 ♡♡♡♡♡♡♡
8 ♡♡♡♡♡♡♡
9 ♡♡♡♡♡♡♡
10 ♡♡♡♡♡♡♡
11 ♡♡♡♡♡♡♡
12 ♡♡♡♡♡♡♡
13 ♡♡♡♡♡♡♡
14 ♡♡♡♡♡♡♡
15 ♡♡♡♡♡♡♡

16 ♡♡♡♡♡♡♡
17 ♡♡♡♡♡♡♡
18 ♡♡♡♡♡♡♡
19 ♡♡♡♡♡♡♡
20 ♡♡♡♡♡♡♡
21 ♡♡♡♡♡♡♡
22 ♡♡♡♡♡♡♡
23 ♡♡♡♡♡♡♡
24 ♡♡♡♡♡♡♡
25 ♡♡♡♡♡♡♡
26 ♡♡♡♡♡♡♡
27 ♡♡♡♡♡♡♡
28 ♡♡♡♡♡♡♡
29 ♡♡♡♡♡♡♡
30 ♡♡♡♡♡♡♡
31 ♡♡♡♡♡♡♡

Media Tracker

Use this page to track the books you've read
and the TV shows and films you've watched
this month and your rating out of five.

Books read this month:

_____ ☆☆☆☆☆

_____ ☆☆☆☆☆

_____ ☆☆☆☆☆

_____ ☆☆☆☆☆

_____ ☆☆☆☆☆

_____ ☆☆☆☆☆

Films and TV shows watched this month:

_____ ☆☆☆☆☆

_____ ☆☆☆☆☆

_____ ☆☆☆☆☆

_____ ☆☆☆☆☆

_____ ☆☆☆☆☆

_____ ☆☆☆☆☆

I have learned that as long as I hold fast to my beliefs and values – and follow my own moral compass – then the only expectations I need to live up to are my own.

MICHELLE OBAMA

June

MY GOALS AND ACHIEVEMENTS

My goal(s) for this month:

Example goal: Eat five portions of fruit and veg every day

_____

_____

_____

What will I do to reach my goal(s)?

Example steps: Start making breakfast smoothies,
create weekly meal planners to make sure vegetables
are included, replace lunchtime crisps or chocolate
with fruit

_____

_____

_____

_____

Top Tips

HOW TO DEAL WITH SETBACKS

If you've been filling out these trackers for a few months, you may have noticed ups and downs when it comes to your success. Sometimes we set goals and we fail, sometimes we take second place when we wanted first, sometimes we come dead last.

Setbacks and failures are a part of life. The only people who never fail at anything are the people who don't try. It's easy to be a success if you always stick to what you're good at or if you don't try new things, set yourself new challenges or step outside your comfort zone. But where's the fun in that?

If you turn down the things that are difficult, that don't come naturally to you, that you'd describe as your weaknesses, you might well project an appearance of never failing, but you will stagnate. Growth comes from trying and failing, from getting it wrong and learning and trying again and again until you get it right. So, celebrate your failures, learn from them, then pick yourself up and try again. You got this.

Spending Tracker

MONTH: JUNE

SURVIVAL		CULTURE	
Food shop	42.35	Cinema	11.95

SURVIVAL: Regular, necessary expenditure, such as food, childcare or transport.

CULTURE: Expenditure on cultural activities, theatre, books, etc.

Total income per month: _____

Income minus fixed costs:_____

OPTIONAL		EXTRA	
Dinner Out	23.27	B-day card	2.50

OPTIONAL: Anything you choose to spend money on, like a social event or meal out.

EXTRA: Anything irregular or unexpected, such as repairs or birthday presents.

Water Tracker

One drop = one glass (400 ml)

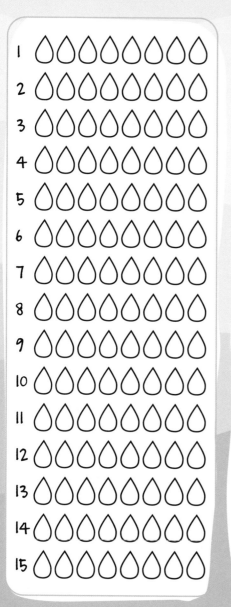

1 ◊◊◊◊◊◊◊
2 ◊◊◊◊◊◊◊
3 ◊◊◊◊◊◊◊
4 ◊◊◊◊◊◊◊
5 ◊◊◊◊◊◊◊
6 ◊◊◊◊◊◊◊
7 ◊◊◊◊◊◊◊
8 ◊◊◊◊◊◊◊
9 ◊◊◊◊◊◊◊
10 ◊◊◊◊◊◊◊
11 ◊◊◊◊◊◊◊
12 ◊◊◊◊◊◊◊
13 ◊◊◊◊◊◊◊
14 ◊◊◊◊◊◊◊
15 ◊◊◊◊◊◊◊

16 ◊◊◊◊◊◊◊
17 ◊◊◊◊◊◊◊
18 ◊◊◊◊◊◊◊
19 ◊◊◊◊◊◊◊
20 ◊◊◊◊◊◊◊
21 ◊◊◊◊◊◊◊
22 ◊◊◊◊◊◊◊
23 ◊◊◊◊◊◊◊
24 ◊◊◊◊◊◊◊
25 ◊◊◊◊◊◊◊
26 ◊◊◊◊◊◊◊
27 ◊◊◊◊◊◊◊
28 ◊◊◊◊◊◊◊
29 ◊◊◊◊◊◊◊
30 ◊◊◊◊◊◊◊

Sleep Tracker

KEY

- ◯ Four hours or fewer
- ◯ Five hours
- ◯ Six hours
- ◯ Seven hours
- ◯ Eight hours
- ◯ Nine hours or more

Exercise Tracker

Use this page to log your activity levels this month.
Write in the number of active minutes for each day
or colour-code each box.

1	2	3	4
5	6	7	8
9	10	11	12
13	14	15	16
17	18	19	20
21	22	23	24
25	26	27	28
29	30		

Active
Moderate
Rest

Mindfulness Tracker

If you had a moment of mindfulness today, record it here by colouring in the spiral.

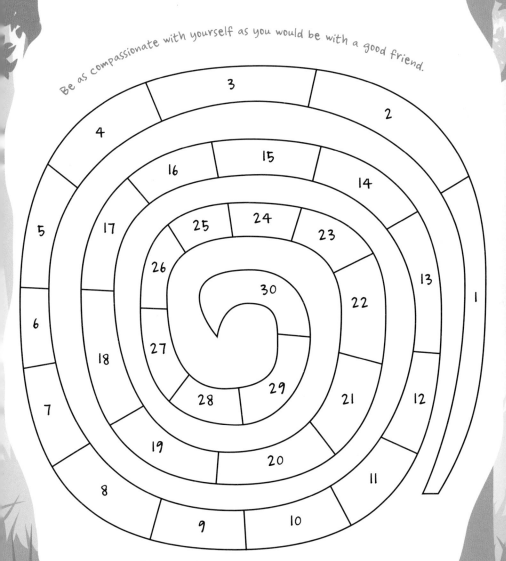

Be as compassionate with yourself as you would be with a good friend.

Make time to enjoy your own company.

Mood Tracker

Great   Good   Average   Poor   Terrible

Social Media Tracker

One heart = 30 minutes

1 ♡♡♡♡♡♡♡
2 ♡♡♡♡♡♡♡
3 ♡♡♡♡♡♡♡
4 ♡♡♡♡♡♡♡
5 ♡♡♡♡♡♡♡
6 ♡♡♡♡♡♡♡
7 ♡♡♡♡♡♡♡
8 ♡♡♡♡♡♡♡
9 ♡♡♡♡♡♡♡
10 ♡♡♡♡♡♡♡
11 ♡♡♡♡♡♡♡
12 ♡♡♡♡♡♡♡
13 ♡♡♡♡♡♡♡
14 ♡♡♡♡♡♡♡
15 ♡♡♡♡♡♡♡

16 ♡♡♡♡♡♡♡
17 ♡♡♡♡♡♡♡
18 ♡♡♡♡♡♡♡
19 ♡♡♡♡♡♡♡
20 ♡♡♡♡♡♡♡
21 ♡♡♡♡♡♡♡
22 ♡♡♡♡♡♡♡
23 ♡♡♡♡♡♡♡
24 ♡♡♡♡♡♡♡
25 ♡♡♡♡♡♡♡
26 ♡♡♡♡♡♡♡
27 ♡♡♡♡♡♡♡
28 ♡♡♡♡♡♡♡
29 ♡♡♡♡♡♡♡
30 ♡♡♡♡♡♡♡

Media Tracker

Use this page to track the books you've read
and the TV shows and films you've watched
this month and your rating out of five.

Books read this month:

_____ ☆☆☆☆☆
_____ ☆☆☆☆☆
_____ ☆☆☆☆☆
_____ ☆☆☆☆☆
_____ ☆☆☆☆☆
_____ ☆☆☆☆☆

Films and TV shows watched this month:

_____ ☆☆☆☆☆
_____ ☆☆☆☆☆
_____ ☆☆☆☆☆
_____ ☆☆☆☆☆
_____ ☆☆☆☆☆
_____ ☆☆☆☆☆

I AM NOT DEFINED
BY MY FAILURES;
I AM DEFINED BY
MY CHARACTER

July

MY GOALS AND ACHIEVEMENTS

My goal(s) for this month:

Example goal: Drink 2 litres of water every day

_____

_____

_____

What will I do to reach my goal(s)?

Example steps: Buy a 1-litre water bottle, set
reminders to drink throughout the day, make sure
the first bottle is finished by lunchtime and refill,
use the water trackers to log my progress

_____

_____

_____

_____

Top Tips

STAY HYDRATED

Up to 70 per cent of our body is water, so to stay healthy we need to make sure we keep hydrated. You should aim to drink between 2 and 2.5 litres of fluid a day – that's roughly eight glasses of water.

If you're not keen on plain water, you can add a slice of lemon, lime, cucumber or some berries. Any non-alcoholic drink contributes towards your goal; just be careful about your sugar intake. You may have heard that caffeinated drinks don't count because they have a diuretic effect (they make you urinate more), but if you stick within the recommended limit – 400 mg a day (one cup of tea contains about 50 mg and one cup of coffee about 90 mg) – it won't be a problem.

Don't wait until you are thirsty to drink – try carrying a water bottle around with you and sip from it throughout the day. You can also get hydration from food; cucumber, celery, grapes and watermelon all have a high water content, but should be eaten in addition to the recommended intake for an extra hydration boost. Sometimes our bodies confuse thirst and hunger, so when you feel hungry try having a drink first.

And remember, if you're exercising, or ill, or the weather is hot, you will need extra hydration.

Spending Tracker

SURVIVAL		CULTURE	
Food shop	42.35	Cinema	11.95

SURVIVAL: Regular, necessary expenditure, such as food, childcare or transport.

CULTURE: Expenditure on cultural activities, theatre, books, etc.

Total income per month: _____

Income minus fixed costs:_____

OPTIONAL		EXTRA	
Dinner Out	23.27	B-day card	2.50

OPTIONAL: Anything you choose to spend money on, like a social event or meal out.

EXTRA: Anything irregular or unexpected, such as repairs or birthday presents.

Water Tracker

One drop = one glass (400 ml)

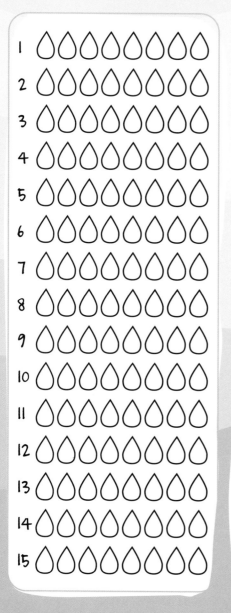

1 ⬠⬠⬠⬠⬠⬠⬠⬠
2 ⬠⬠⬠⬠⬠⬠⬠⬠
3 ⬠⬠⬠⬠⬠⬠⬠⬠
4 ⬠⬠⬠⬠⬠⬠⬠⬠
5 ⬠⬠⬠⬠⬠⬠⬠⬠
6 ⬠⬠⬠⬠⬠⬠⬠⬠
7 ⬠⬠⬠⬠⬠⬠⬠⬠
8 ⬠⬠⬠⬠⬠⬠⬠⬠
9 ⬠⬠⬠⬠⬠⬠⬠⬠
10 ⬠⬠⬠⬠⬠⬠⬠⬠
11 ⬠⬠⬠⬠⬠⬠⬠⬠
12 ⬠⬠⬠⬠⬠⬠⬠⬠
13 ⬠⬠⬠⬠⬠⬠⬠⬠
14 ⬠⬠⬠⬠⬠⬠⬠⬠
15 ⬠⬠⬠⬠⬠⬠⬠⬠

16 ⬠⬠⬠⬠⬠⬠⬠⬠
17 ⬠⬠⬠⬠⬠⬠⬠⬠
18 ⬠⬠⬠⬠⬠⬠⬠⬠
19 ⬠⬠⬠⬠⬠⬠⬠⬠
20 ⬠⬠⬠⬠⬠⬠⬠⬠
21 ⬠⬠⬠⬠⬠⬠⬠⬠
22 ⬠⬠⬠⬠⬠⬠⬠⬠
23 ⬠⬠⬠⬠⬠⬠⬠⬠
24 ⬠⬠⬠⬠⬠⬠⬠⬠
25 ⬠⬠⬠⬠⬠⬠⬠⬠
26 ⬠⬠⬠⬠⬠⬠⬠⬠
27 ⬠⬠⬠⬠⬠⬠⬠⬠
28 ⬠⬠⬠⬠⬠⬠⬠⬠
29 ⬠⬠⬠⬠⬠⬠⬠⬠
30 ⬠⬠⬠⬠⬠⬠⬠⬠
31 ⬠⬠⬠⬠⬠⬠⬠⬠

Sleep Tracker

KEY

- ☐ Four hours or fewer
- ☐ Five hours
- ☐ Six hours
- ☐ Seven hours
- ☐ Eight hours
- ☐ Nine hours or more

Exercise Tracker

Use this page to log your activity levels this month.
Write in the number of active minutes for each day
or colour-code each box.

1	2	3	4
5	6	7	8
9	10	11	12
13	14	15	16
17	18	19	20
21	22	23	24
25	26	27	28
29	30	31	

○ Active
○ Moderate
○ Rest

Mindfulness Tracker

If you had a moment of mindfulness today, record it here by colouring in the spiral.

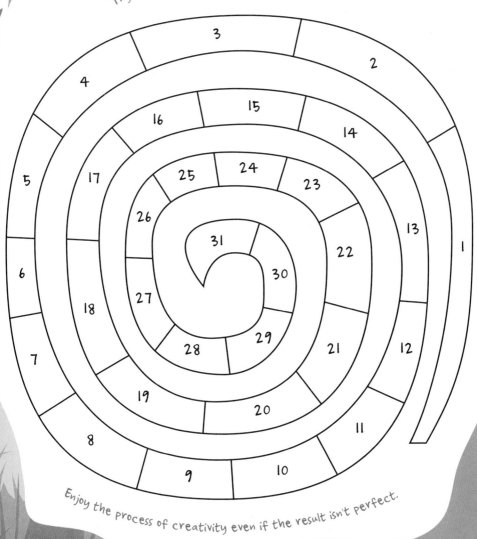

Try a mindfulness colouring book or jigsaw.

Enjoy the process of creativity even if the result isn't perfect.

Mood Tracker

Great Good Average Poor Terrible

Social Media Tracker

One heart = 30 minutes

1 ♡♡♡♡♡♡♡
2 ♡♡♡♡♡♡♡
3 ♡♡♡♡♡♡♡
4 ♡♡♡♡♡♡♡
5 ♡♡♡♡♡♡♡
6 ♡♡♡♡♡♡♡
7 ♡♡♡♡♡♡♡
8 ♡♡♡♡♡♡♡
9 ♡♡♡♡♡♡♡
10 ♡♡♡♡♡♡♡
11 ♡♡♡♡♡♡♡
12 ♡♡♡♡♡♡♡
13 ♡♡♡♡♡♡♡
14 ♡♡♡♡♡♡♡
15 ♡♡♡♡♡♡♡

16 ♡♡♡♡♡♡♡
17 ♡♡♡♡♡♡♡
18 ♡♡♡♡♡♡♡
19 ♡♡♡♡♡♡♡
20 ♡♡♡♡♡♡♡
21 ♡♡♡♡♡♡♡
22 ♡♡♡♡♡♡♡
23 ♡♡♡♡♡♡♡
24 ♡♡♡♡♡♡♡
25 ♡♡♡♡♡♡♡
26 ♡♡♡♡♡♡♡
27 ♡♡♡♡♡♡♡
28 ♡♡♡♡♡♡♡
29 ♡♡♡♡♡♡♡
30 ♡♡♡♡♡♡♡
31 ♡♡♡♡♡♡♡

Media Tracker

Use this page to track the books you've read and the TV shows and films you've watched this month and your rating out of five.

Books read this month:

_____ ☆☆☆☆☆

_____ ☆☆☆☆☆

_____ ☆☆☆☆☆

_____ ☆☆☆☆☆

_____ ☆☆☆☆☆

_____ ☆☆☆☆☆

Films and TV shows watched this month:

_____ ☆☆☆☆☆

_____ ☆☆☆☆☆

_____ ☆☆☆☆☆

_____ ☆☆☆☆☆

_____ ☆☆☆☆☆

_____ ☆☆☆☆☆

The only one who can
tell you "you can't win"
is you and you don't
have to listen.

JESSICA ENNIS-HILL

August

MY GOALS AND ACHIEVEMENTS

My goal(s) for this month:

Example goal: Cut social media use by half

_____

_____

_____

What will I do to reach my goal(s)?

Example steps: Turn off notifications, set screen-time limits on phone, put my phone away in another room when relaxing in the evening

_____

_____

_____

_____

_____

Top Tips

SOCIAL MEDIA: FRIEND OR FOE?

Social media can be great for reuniting people with their lost pets, helping us keep in touch with distant relatives, encouraging acts of kindness, and so much more.

It also has pitfalls. Social commentators have recently identified the phenomenon of "doomscrolling": spending a long time scrolling through social media absorbing one piece of bad news after another. Psychologists warn that this can lead to increased anxiety levels and can even produce symptoms of post-traumatic stress disorder (PTSD), so it's best to try to keep your social media bubble happy and positive.

Another pitfall is comparison. Most of us are inclined to present our best self in public and this is enhanced on social media, which is full of cheesy hashtags, humble brags and heavily filtered photos that hide our imperfections. The problem is we forget that everyone else is doing the same thing. We may see our friend's workout schedule or perfect family photos and feel that we aren't quite enough. Remember, we're comparing our normal to others' heavily edited Instagram life. So put down your phone and start enjoying the life you want to live.

Spending Tracker

MONTH: AUGUST

SURVIVAL		CULTURE	
Food shop	42.35	Cinema	11.95

SURVIVAL: Regular, necessary expenditure, such as food, childcare or transport.

CULTURE: Expenditure on cultural activities, theatre, books, etc.

Total income per month: _____

Income minus fixed costs: _____

OPTIONAL		EXTRA	
Dinner Out	23.27	B-day card	2.50

OPTIONAL: Anything you choose to spend money on, like a social event or meal out.

EXTRA: Anything irregular or unexpected, such as repairs or birthday presents.

Water Tracker

One drop = one glass (400 ml)

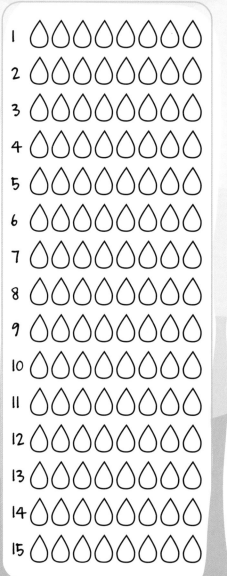

1 ⬩⬩⬩⬩⬩⬩⬩⬩
2 ⬩⬩⬩⬩⬩⬩⬩⬩
3 ⬩⬩⬩⬩⬩⬩⬩⬩
4 ⬩⬩⬩⬩⬩⬩⬩⬩
5 ⬩⬩⬩⬩⬩⬩⬩⬩
6 ⬩⬩⬩⬩⬩⬩⬩⬩
7 ⬩⬩⬩⬩⬩⬩⬩⬩
8 ⬩⬩⬩⬩⬩⬩⬩⬩
9 ⬩⬩⬩⬩⬩⬩⬩⬩
10 ⬩⬩⬩⬩⬩⬩⬩⬩
11 ⬩⬩⬩⬩⬩⬩⬩⬩
12 ⬩⬩⬩⬩⬩⬩⬩⬩
13 ⬩⬩⬩⬩⬩⬩⬩⬩
14 ⬩⬩⬩⬩⬩⬩⬩⬩
15 ⬩⬩⬩⬩⬩⬩⬩⬩

16 ⬩⬩⬩⬩⬩⬩⬩⬩
17 ⬩⬩⬩⬩⬩⬩⬩⬩
18 ⬩⬩⬩⬩⬩⬩⬩⬩
19 ⬩⬩⬩⬩⬩⬩⬩⬩
20 ⬩⬩⬩⬩⬩⬩⬩⬩
21 ⬩⬩⬩⬩⬩⬩⬩⬩
22 ⬩⬩⬩⬩⬩⬩⬩⬩
23 ⬩⬩⬩⬩⬩⬩⬩⬩
24 ⬩⬩⬩⬩⬩⬩⬩⬩
25 ⬩⬩⬩⬩⬩⬩⬩⬩
26 ⬩⬩⬩⬩⬩⬩⬩⬩
27 ⬩⬩⬩⬩⬩⬩⬩⬩
28 ⬩⬩⬩⬩⬩⬩⬩⬩
29 ⬩⬩⬩⬩⬩⬩⬩⬩
30 ⬩⬩⬩⬩⬩⬩⬩⬩
31 ⬩⬩⬩⬩⬩⬩⬩⬩

Sleep Tracker

KEY

- ☐ Four hours or fewer
- ☐ Five hours
- ☐ Six hours
- ☐ Seven hours
- ☐ Eight hours
- ☐ Nine hours or more

Exercise Tracker

Use this page to log your activity levels this month.
Write in the number of active minutes for each day
or colour-code each box.

1	2	3	4
5	6	7	8
9	10	11	12
13	14	15	16
17	18	19	20
21	22	23	24
25	26	27	28
29	30	31	

◯ Active
◯ Moderate
◯ Rest

Mindfulness Tracker

If you had a moment of mindfulness today, record it here by colouring in the spiral.

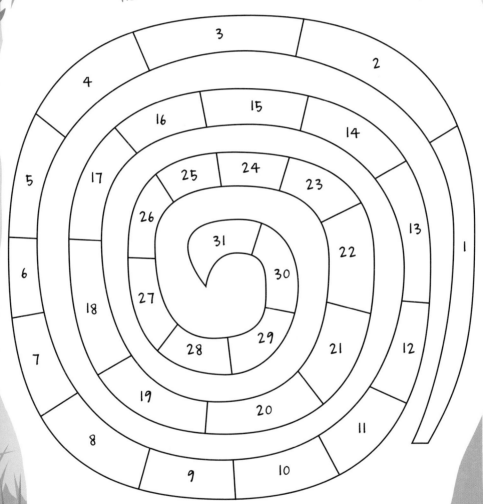

Acknowledge and accept your feelings.

Practise naming your emotions as they arise.

Mood Tracker

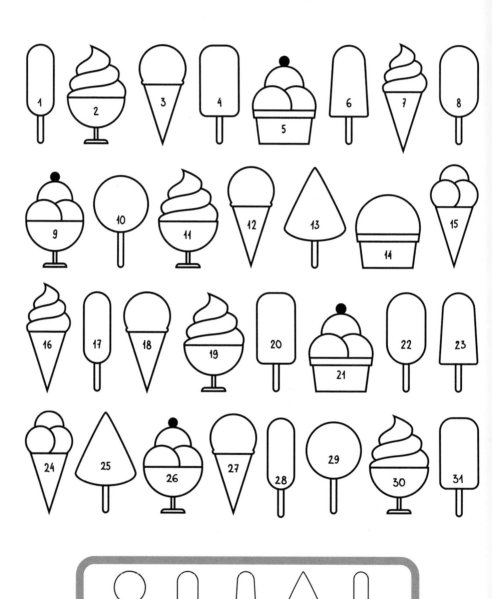

Social Media Tracker

One heart = 30 minutes

1 ♡♡♡♡♡♡♡
2 ♡♡♡♡♡♡♡
3 ♡♡♡♡♡♡♡
4 ♡♡♡♡♡♡♡
5 ♡♡♡♡♡♡♡
6 ♡♡♡♡♡♡♡
7 ♡♡♡♡♡♡♡
8 ♡♡♡♡♡♡♡
9 ♡♡♡♡♡♡♡
10 ♡♡♡♡♡♡♡
11 ♡♡♡♡♡♡♡
12 ♡♡♡♡♡♡♡
13 ♡♡♡♡♡♡♡
14 ♡♡♡♡♡♡♡
15 ♡♡♡♡♡♡♡

16 ♡♡♡♡♡♡♡
17 ♡♡♡♡♡♡♡
18 ♡♡♡♡♡♡♡
19 ♡♡♡♡♡♡♡
20 ♡♡♡♡♡♡♡
21 ♡♡♡♡♡♡♡
22 ♡♡♡♡♡♡♡
23 ♡♡♡♡♡♡♡
24 ♡♡♡♡♡♡♡
25 ♡♡♡♡♡♡♡
26 ♡♡♡♡♡♡♡
27 ♡♡♡♡♡♡♡
28 ♡♡♡♡♡♡♡
29 ♡♡♡♡♡♡♡
30 ♡♡♡♡♡♡♡
31 ♡♡♡♡♡♡♡

Media Tracker

Use this page to track the books you've read
and the TV shows and films you've watched
this month and your rating out of five.

Books read this month:

_____ ☆☆☆☆☆

_____ ☆☆☆☆☆

_____ ☆☆☆☆☆

_____ ☆☆☆☆☆

_____ ☆☆☆☆☆

_____ ☆☆☆☆☆

Films and TV shows watched this month:

_____ ☆☆☆☆☆

_____ ☆☆☆☆☆

_____ ☆☆☆☆☆

_____ ☆☆☆☆☆

_____ ☆☆☆☆☆

_____ ☆☆☆☆☆

I AM A UNIQUE INDIVIDUAL, INCOMPARABLE TO ANYONE ELSE

September

MY GOALS AND ACHIEVEMENTS

My goal(s) for this month:

Example goal: Eat a healthy, home-cooked meal four out of seven nights per week

_____

_____

_____

What will I do to reach my goal(s)?

Example steps: Make a meal plan each week, buy all the ingredients at the start of each week, batch cook in the first week of the month and freeze meals, so they can be reheated on busy days

_____

_____

_____

Top Tips

THE FIVE-MINUTE PAUSE

Mindfulness is a state of awareness, being calm and fully present in the moment, and with time and practice, it will become something you don't have to remember to do. However, in the fray of a stressful day, it's easy to forget to practise mindfulness as we lose track of time, become lost in our feelings and overthink.

This is where the five-minute pause comes in. Throughout the day, get into the habit of stopping for five minutes to recharge. You don't need to do anything complicated – just close your eyes and focus on slowing your breathing. Or perhaps ground yourself by noticing your surroundings, your bodily sensations and your emotions. You might want to spend five minutes with your eyes closed lying on your favourite beach (in your mind) or listen intently to your favourite song, noticing all the different instruments and tones. You could try reading something upbeat and positive, meditating on each word as you go, or just slowly savour the taste of a chocolate biscuit or juicy apple.

If you need some assistance to begin with, there are lots of five-minute guided meditation videos available free online. Allow yourself regular breathing space, rediscover your equilibrium and then approach the rest of the day with cool confidence.

Spending Tracker

MONTH: SEPTEMBER

SURVIVAL		CULTURE	
Food shop	42.35	Cinema	11.95

SURVIVAL: Regular, necessary expenditure, such as food, childcare or transport.

CULTURE: Expenditure on cultural activities, theatre, books, etc.

Total income per month: _____

Income minus fixed costs: _____

OPTIONAL		EXTRA	
Dinner Out	23.27	B-day card	2.50

OPTIONAL: Anything you choose to spend money on, like a social event or meal out.

EXTRA: Anything irregular or unexpected, such as repairs or birthday presents.

Water Tracker

One drop = one glass (400 ml)

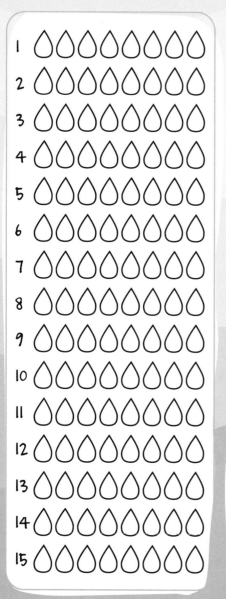

1 ⬦⬦⬦⬦⬦⬦⬦
2 ⬦⬦⬦⬦⬦⬦⬦
3 ⬦⬦⬦⬦⬦⬦⬦
4 ⬦⬦⬦⬦⬦⬦⬦
5 ⬦⬦⬦⬦⬦⬦⬦
6 ⬦⬦⬦⬦⬦⬦⬦
7 ⬦⬦⬦⬦⬦⬦⬦
8 ⬦⬦⬦⬦⬦⬦⬦
9 ⬦⬦⬦⬦⬦⬦⬦
10 ⬦⬦⬦⬦⬦⬦⬦
11 ⬦⬦⬦⬦⬦⬦⬦
12 ⬦⬦⬦⬦⬦⬦⬦
13 ⬦⬦⬦⬦⬦⬦⬦
14 ⬦⬦⬦⬦⬦⬦⬦
15 ⬦⬦⬦⬦⬦⬦⬦

16 ⬦⬦⬦⬦⬦⬦⬦
17 ⬦⬦⬦⬦⬦⬦⬦
18 ⬦⬦⬦⬦⬦⬦⬦
19 ⬦⬦⬦⬦⬦⬦⬦
20 ⬦⬦⬦⬦⬦⬦⬦
21 ⬦⬦⬦⬦⬦⬦⬦
22 ⬦⬦⬦⬦⬦⬦⬦
23 ⬦⬦⬦⬦⬦⬦⬦
24 ⬦⬦⬦⬦⬦⬦⬦
25 ⬦⬦⬦⬦⬦⬦⬦
26 ⬦⬦⬦⬦⬦⬦⬦
27 ⬦⬦⬦⬦⬦⬦⬦
28 ⬦⬦⬦⬦⬦⬦⬦
29 ⬦⬦⬦⬦⬦⬦⬦
30 ⬦⬦⬦⬦⬦⬦⬦

Sleep Tracker

KEY

- ☐ Four hours or fewer
- ☐ Five hours
- ☐ Six hours
- ☐ Seven hours
- ☐ Eight hours
- ☐ Nine hours or more

Exercise Tracker

Use this page to log your activity levels this month.
Write in the number of active minutes for each day
or colour-code each box.

1	2	3	4
5	6	7	8
9	10	11	12
13	14	15	16
17	18	19	20
21	22	23	24
25	26	27	28
29	30		

Active
Moderate
Rest

Mindfulness Tracker

If you had a moment of mindfulness today, record it here by colouring in the spiral.

Focus on your breathing for a few minutes.
Breathe in and out through your nose for five counts each.

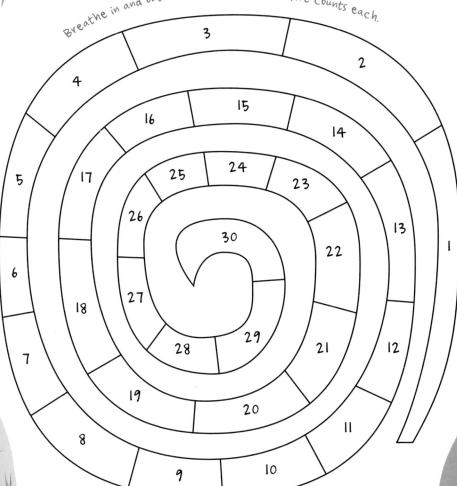

As you breathe in, feel the breath fill your lungs.

Mood Tracker

Great Good Average Poor Terrible

Social Media Tracker

One heart = 30 minutes

1 ♡♡♡♡♡♡♡
2 ♡♡♡♡♡♡♡
3 ♡♡♡♡♡♡♡
4 ♡♡♡♡♡♡♡
5 ♡♡♡♡♡♡♡
6 ♡♡♡♡♡♡♡
7 ♡♡♡♡♡♡♡
8 ♡♡♡♡♡♡♡
9 ♡♡♡♡♡♡♡
10 ♡♡♡♡♡♡♡
11 ♡♡♡♡♡♡♡
12 ♡♡♡♡♡♡♡
13 ♡♡♡♡♡♡♡
14 ♡♡♡♡♡♡♡
15 ♡♡♡♡♡♡♡

16 ♡♡♡♡♡♡♡
17 ♡♡♡♡♡♡♡
18 ♡♡♡♡♡♡♡
19 ♡♡♡♡♡♡♡
20 ♡♡♡♡♡♡♡
21 ♡♡♡♡♡♡♡
22 ♡♡♡♡♡♡♡
23 ♡♡♡♡♡♡♡
24 ♡♡♡♡♡♡♡
25 ♡♡♡♡♡♡♡
26 ♡♡♡♡♡♡♡
27 ♡♡♡♡♡♡♡
28 ♡♡♡♡♡♡♡
29 ♡♡♡♡♡♡♡
30 ♡♡♡♡♡♡♡

Media Tracker

Use this page to track the books you've read and the TV shows and films you've watched this month and your rating out of five.

Books read this month:

_____ ☆☆☆☆☆

_____ ☆☆☆☆☆

_____ ☆☆☆☆☆

_____ ☆☆☆☆☆

_____ ☆☆☆☆☆

_____ ☆☆☆☆☆

Films and TV shows watched this month:

_____ ☆☆☆☆☆

_____ ☆☆☆☆☆

_____ ☆☆☆☆☆

_____ ☆☆☆☆☆

_____ ☆☆☆☆☆

_____ ☆☆☆☆☆

Almost everything
will work again if
you unplug it for a few
minutes, including you.

ANNE LAMOTT

October

MY GOALS AND ACHIEVEMENTS

My goal(s) for this month:

Example goal: Establish a healthier sleeping pattern

_____

_____

_____

What will I do to reach my goal(s)?

Example steps: Set a wind-down alarm an hour
before bedtime, stop using any devices during this
hour, start a daily relaxation exercise at bedtime

_____

_____

_____

_____

_____

Top Tips

SLEEP WELL

Most adults need seven to nine hours' sleep each night but only get six to seven. Globally, 62 per cent of people feel they aren't getting enough sleep. Getting less than six hours' sleep a night is associated with a host of health problems, while conversely, science tells us that those who sleep well are physically, emotionally and mentally healthier. In order to function properly, sleep is essential.

Establish a good routine by going to bed and getting up at around the same time each day. Use an alarm to remind you to wind down and switch off your screens an hour before you go to bed. Avoiding caffeine and large meals in the evenings will also help you to sleep better, as will making sure you get plenty of fresh air and exercise during the day.

Stress and anxiety can hinder healthy sleep, and this creates a vicious circle because not getting enough sleep makes it more difficult to cope with stress and anxiety. Try to focus your mind on something relaxing before you go to bed: give meditation or relaxation exercises a go, listen to some relaxing music or immerse yourself in a book.

Spending Tracker

MONTH: OCTOBER

SURVIVAL		CULTURE	
Food shop	42.35	Cinema	11.95

SURVIVAL: Regular, necessary expenditure, such as food, childcare or transport.

CULTURE: Expenditure on cultural activities, theatre, books, etc.

Total income per month: _____

Income minus fixed costs: _____

OPTIONAL		EXTRA	
Dinner Out	23.27	B-day card	2.50

OPTIONAL: Anything you choose to spend money on, like a social event or meal out.

EXTRA: Anything irregular or unexpected, such as repairs or birthday presents.

Water Tracker

One drop = one glass (400 ml)

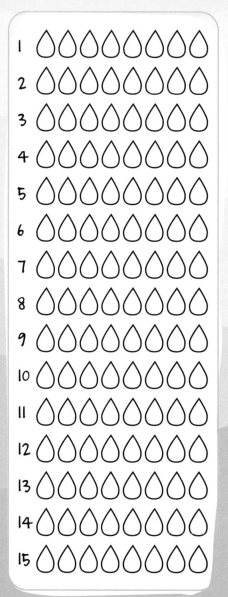

Sleep Tracker

KEY

- ◯ Four hours or fewer
- ◯ Six hours
- ◯ Eight hours
- ◯ Five hours
- ◯ Seven hours
- ◯ Nine hours or more

Exercise Tracker

Use this page to log your activity levels this month.
Write in the number of active minutes for each day
or colour-code each box.

1	2	3	4
5	6	7	8
9	10	11	12
13	14	15	16
17	18	19	20
21	22	23	24
25	26	27	28
29	30	31	

Active
Moderate
Rest

Mindfulness Tracker

If you had a moment of mindfulness today, record it here by colouring in the spiral.

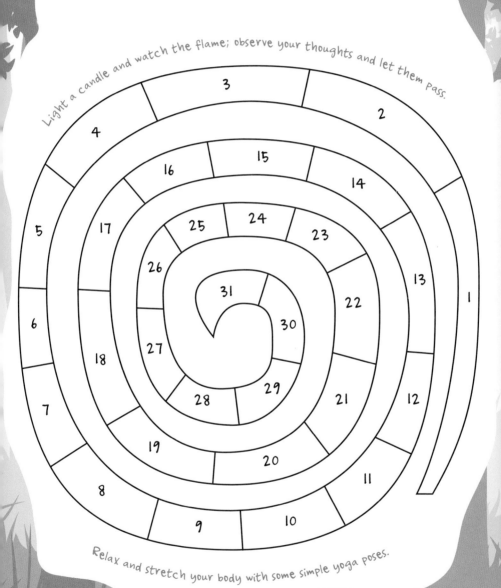

Light a candle and watch the flame; observe your thoughts and let them pass.

Relax and stretch your body with some simple yoga poses.

Mood Tracker

Great   Good   Average   Poor   Terrible

Social Media Tracker

One heart = 30 minutes

1 ♡ ♡ ♡ ♡ ♡ ♡ ♡
2 ♡ ♡ ♡ ♡ ♡ ♡ ♡
3 ♡ ♡ ♡ ♡ ♡ ♡ ♡
4 ♡ ♡ ♡ ♡ ♡ ♡ ♡
5 ♡ ♡ ♡ ♡ ♡ ♡ ♡
6 ♡ ♡ ♡ ♡ ♡ ♡ ♡
7 ♡ ♡ ♡ ♡ ♡ ♡ ♡
8 ♡ ♡ ♡ ♡ ♡ ♡ ♡
9 ♡ ♡ ♡ ♡ ♡ ♡ ♡
10 ♡ ♡ ♡ ♡ ♡ ♡ ♡
11 ♡ ♡ ♡ ♡ ♡ ♡ ♡
12 ♡ ♡ ♡ ♡ ♡ ♡ ♡
13 ♡ ♡ ♡ ♡ ♡ ♡ ♡
14 ♡ ♡ ♡ ♡ ♡ ♡ ♡
15 ♡ ♡ ♡ ♡ ♡ ♡ ♡

16 ♡ ♡ ♡ ♡ ♡ ♡ ♡
17 ♡ ♡ ♡ ♡ ♡ ♡ ♡
18 ♡ ♡ ♡ ♡ ♡ ♡ ♡
19 ♡ ♡ ♡ ♡ ♡ ♡ ♡
20 ♡ ♡ ♡ ♡ ♡ ♡ ♡
21 ♡ ♡ ♡ ♡ ♡ ♡ ♡
22 ♡ ♡ ♡ ♡ ♡ ♡ ♡
23 ♡ ♡ ♡ ♡ ♡ ♡ ♡
24 ♡ ♡ ♡ ♡ ♡ ♡ ♡
25 ♡ ♡ ♡ ♡ ♡ ♡ ♡
26 ♡ ♡ ♡ ♡ ♡ ♡ ♡
27 ♡ ♡ ♡ ♡ ♡ ♡ ♡
28 ♡ ♡ ♡ ♡ ♡ ♡ ♡
29 ♡ ♡ ♡ ♡ ♡ ♡ ♡
30 ♡ ♡ ♡ ♡ ♡ ♡ ♡
31 ♡ ♡ ♡ ♡ ♡ ♡ ♡

Media Tracker

Use this page to track the books you've read
and the TV shows and films you've watched
this month and your rating out of five.

Books read this month:

_____ ☆☆☆☆☆
_____ ☆☆☆☆☆
_____ ☆☆☆☆☆
_____ ☆☆☆☆☆
_____ ☆☆☆☆☆
_____ ☆☆☆☆☆

Films and TV shows watched this month:

_____ ☆☆☆☆☆
_____ ☆☆☆☆☆
_____ ☆☆☆☆☆
_____ ☆☆☆☆☆
_____ ☆☆☆☆☆
_____ ☆☆☆☆☆

GOOD HEALTH
IS THE FOUNDATION
OF SUCCESS

November

MY GOALS AND ACHIEVEMENTS

My goal(s) for this month:

Example goal: Reduce my spending

What will I do to reach my goal(s)?

Example steps: Put a freeze on my credit cards, start taking a flask out instead of buying takeaway coffee, review spending each day

Top Tips

HOW TO AVOID OVERSPENDING

Overspending is an easy habit to fall into but one that can be broken with some small, simple changes. Here are some ways to cut back on expenditure:

- Skip takeaways: Take a flask of coffee and a packed lunch to work. Plan your meals and make a shopping list – this will reduce impulse buying.

- Make a budget and stick to it: Work out how much you can afford to spend each week. Use your tracker to help you stick to this. Once it's gone, it's gone.

- Mull it over: If there's something you think you really want, don't just go out and buy it. Wait two weeks to see if you still want it; sometimes you'll realize it was just a passing fancy.

- Set a savings goal and track it: Saving for something specific, having a target to hit and seeing the savings grow will motivate you to be more mindful about where your money is going.

- Re-evaluate your subscriptions: Are you still buying magazines you don't get round to reading or do you subscribe to several on-demand TV services? Do you need them all?

Spending Tracker

SURVIVAL		CULTURE	
Food shop	42.35	Cinema	11.95

SURVIVAL: Regular, necessary expenditure, such as food, childcare or transport.

CULTURE: Expenditure on cultural activities, theatre, books, etc.

Total income per month: _____

Income minus fixed costs:_____

OPTIONAL		EXTRA	
Dinner Out	23.27	B-day card	2.50

OPTIONAL: Anything you choose to spend money on, like a social event or meal out.

EXTRA: Anything irregular or unexpected, such as repairs or birthday presents.

Water Tracker

One drop = one glass (400 ml)

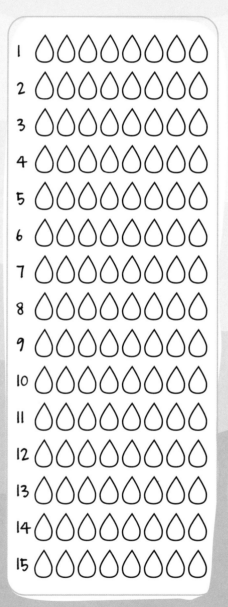

1 ○○○○○○○	16 ○○○○○○○
2 ○○○○○○○	17 ○○○○○○○
3 ○○○○○○○	18 ○○○○○○○
4 ○○○○○○○	19 ○○○○○○○
5 ○○○○○○○	20 ○○○○○○○
6 ○○○○○○○	21 ○○○○○○○
7 ○○○○○○○	22 ○○○○○○○
8 ○○○○○○○	23 ○○○○○○○
9 ○○○○○○○	24 ○○○○○○○
10 ○○○○○○○	25 ○○○○○○○
11 ○○○○○○○	26 ○○○○○○○
12 ○○○○○○○	27 ○○○○○○○
13 ○○○○○○○	28 ○○○○○○○
14 ○○○○○○○	29 ○○○○○○○
15 ○○○○○○○	30 ○○○○○○○

Sleep Tracker

KEY

- ◯ Four hours or fewer
- ◯ Five hours
- ◯ Six hours
- ◯ Seven hours
- ◯ Eight hours
- ◯ Nine hours or more

Exercise Tracker

Use this page to log your activity levels this month. Write in the number of active minutes for each day or colour-code each box.

1

2

3

4

5

6

7

8

9

10

11

12

13

14

15

16

17

18

19

20

21

22

23

24

25

26

27

28

29

30

Active

Moderate

Rest

Mindfulness Tracker

If you had a moment of mindfulness today, record it here by colouring in the spiral.

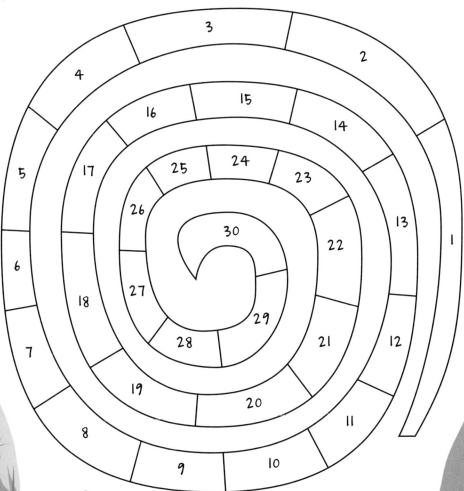

Find joy in simple pleasures.

Spend time outside and notice the breeze on your skin.

Mood Tracker

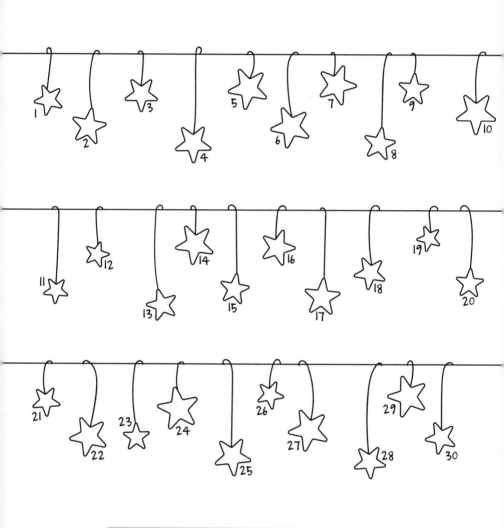

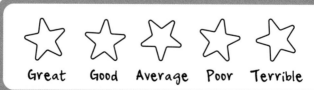

Great   Good   Average   Poor   Terrible

Social Media Tracker

One heart = 30 minutes

1	16
2	17
3	18
4	19
5	20
6	21
7	22
8	23
9	24
10	25
11	26
12	27
13	28
14	29
15	30

Media Tracker

Use this page to track the books you've read and the TV shows and films you've watched this month and your rating out of five.

Books read this month:

_____ ☆☆☆☆☆
_____ ☆☆☆☆☆
_____ ☆☆☆☆☆
_____ ☆☆☆☆☆
_____ ☆☆☆☆☆
_____ ☆☆☆☆☆

Films and TV shows watched this month:

_____ ☆☆☆☆☆
_____ ☆☆☆☆☆
_____ ☆☆☆☆☆
_____ ☆☆☆☆☆
_____ ☆☆☆☆☆
_____ ☆☆☆☆☆

Just remember, you can do anything you set your mind to, but it takes action, perseverance, and facing your fears.

GILLIAN ANDERSON

December

MY GOALS AND ACHIEVEMENTS

My goal(s) for this month:

Example goal: Read two books this month

What will I do to reach my goal(s)?

Example steps: Treat myself to a bookshop trip
to choose books, read a chapter a night, join
Goodreads and start a log

Top Tips

HEALTHY TV HABITS

In moderation, TV could enhance your brainpower, soothe stress and boost happiness. It's all about what you watch, how much you watch and how you watch it.

Choose shows that make you feel good. There are obvious benefits to educational documentaries but feel-good lifestyle programmes, dramas or comedies can also make us feel more positive, more altruistic and less stressed. Conversely, psychologists say that watching reality TV shows full of bickering celebrities can raise our stress levels. Consider how you feel after watching a show: if you don't feel good, don't watch it.

On-demand services mean it's now easier to fit TV around our lives rather than our lives around TV. Choose specific times to watch your favourite shows and then, once they're finished, switch off and do something else. Make TV a social activity: curl up with friends in front of a comedy show and have a good belly laugh together. Shared viewing is great for helping build connections with the people in our lives.

Finally, think about whether you can incorporate exercise into your TV schedule. Do a few star jumps or lunges in front of your favourite show and you'll have burned through those calories before you know it.

Spending Tracker

MONTH: DECEMBER

SURVIVAL		CULTURE	
Food shop	42.35	Cinema	11.95

SURVIVAL: Regular, necessary expenditure, such as food, childcare or transport.

CULTURE: Expenditure on cultural activities, theatre, books, etc.

Total income per month: _____

Income minus fixed costs:_____

OPTIONAL		EXTRA	
Dinner Out	23.27	B-day card	2.50

OPTIONAL: Anything you choose to spend money on, like a social event or meal out.

EXTRA: Anything irregular or unexpected, such as repairs or birthday presents.

Water Tracker

One drop = one glass (400 ml)

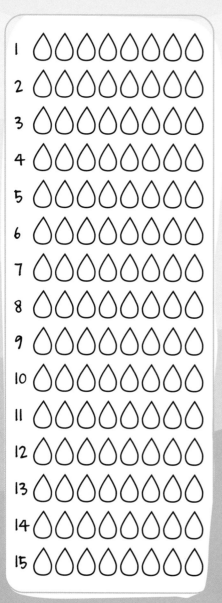

Sleep Tracker

KEY

- ☐ Four hours or fewer
- ☐ Five hours
- ☐ Six hours
- ☐ Seven hours
- ☐ Eight hours
- ☐ Nine hours or more

Exercise Tracker

Use this page to log your activity levels this month.
Write in the number of active minutes for each day
or colour-code each box.

1	2	3	4
5	6	7	8
9	10	11	12
13	14	15	16
17	18	19	20
21	22	23	24
25	26	27	28
29	30	31	

◯ Active
◯ Moderate
◯ Rest

Mindfulness Tracker

If you had a moment of mindfulness today, record it here by colouring in the spiral.

Blow bubbles. Notice the way they float and how the light catches them.

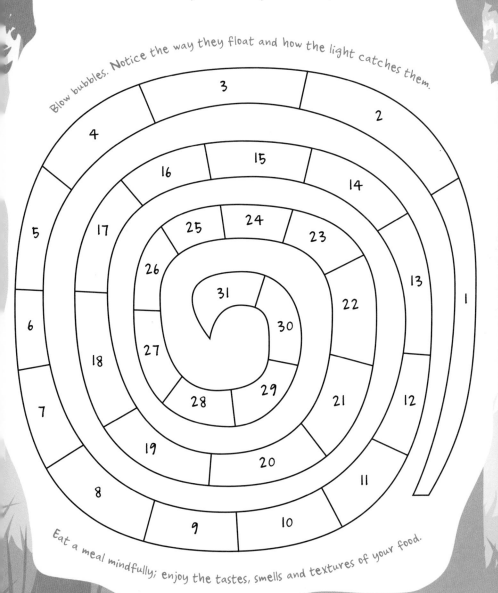

Eat a meal mindfully; enjoy the tastes, smells and textures of your food.

Mood Tracker

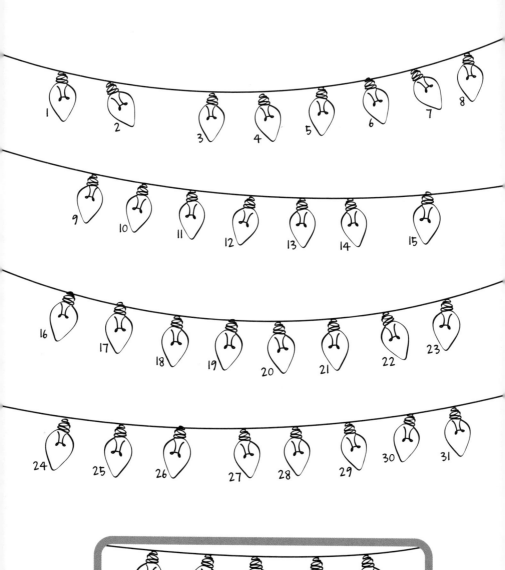

Great   Good   Average   Poor   Terrible

Social Media Tracker

One heart = 30 minutes

1 ♡♡♡♡♡♡♡
2 ♡♡♡♡♡♡♡
3 ♡♡♡♡♡♡♡
4 ♡♡♡♡♡♡♡
5 ♡♡♡♡♡♡♡
6 ♡♡♡♡♡♡♡
7 ♡♡♡♡♡♡♡
8 ♡♡♡♡♡♡♡
9 ♡♡♡♡♡♡♡
10 ♡♡♡♡♡♡♡
11 ♡♡♡♡♡♡♡
12 ♡♡♡♡♡♡♡
13 ♡♡♡♡♡♡♡
14 ♡♡♡♡♡♡♡
15 ♡♡♡♡♡♡♡

16 ♡♡♡♡♡♡♡
17 ♡♡♡♡♡♡♡
18 ♡♡♡♡♡♡♡
19 ♡♡♡♡♡♡♡
20 ♡♡♡♡♡♡♡
21 ♡♡♡♡♡♡♡
22 ♡♡♡♡♡♡♡
23 ♡♡♡♡♡♡♡
24 ♡♡♡♡♡♡♡
25 ♡♡♡♡♡♡♡
26 ♡♡♡♡♡♡♡
27 ♡♡♡♡♡♡♡
28 ♡♡♡♡♡♡♡
29 ♡♡♡♡♡♡♡
30 ♡♡♡♡♡♡♡
31 ♡♡♡♡♡♡♡

Media Tracker

Use this page to track the books you've read and the TV shows and films you've watched this month and your rating out of five.

Books read this month:

_____ ☆☆☆☆☆
_____ ☆☆☆☆☆
_____ ☆☆☆☆☆
_____ ☆☆☆☆☆
_____ ☆☆☆☆☆
_____ ☆☆☆☆☆

Films and TV shows watched this month:

_____ ☆☆☆☆☆
_____ ☆☆☆☆☆
_____ ☆☆☆☆☆
_____ ☆☆☆☆☆
_____ ☆☆☆☆☆
_____ ☆☆☆☆☆

YOU ARE WORTHY OF ALL THE GOOD THINGS LIFE HAS TO OFFER

Conclusion

You've reached the end of your journey and hopefully have a book full of colourful trackers and a year of memories and achievements. You'll have had ups and downs, losses and gains. Sometimes you'll have achieved what you set out to do and other times you won't. For better or worse, you've kept going and spent a whole year living with intention and purpose – not just letting life happen to you, but taking control of your own time, your own well-being and ultimately your own destiny. You deserve a big pat on the back. Well done!

Throughout this process you may have had a goal in mind, or you may just have been curious to find out more about your habits and behaviours. You may have developed new interests, shaken off old unhelpful attitudes or learned to find balance and perspective in how you manage your time. This could have been a remarkable journey of self-discovery or the affirmation you needed that you're on the right track. How has it been? What have you learned? What will you take with you into next year? Now you've viewed the big picture, will you swoop down and hone the detail, and fine-tune a particular aspect of your life? Or will you soar to new heights, set new benchmarks, create new challenges and add more colour to the landscape of your life?

That's all entirely up to you. Next year is your oyster, yours for the taking. Go get it!

Notes

Use this space to reflect on
your life so far.

Also Available

MY HAPPINESS TRACKER
ISBN: 978-1-80007-446-0

MY STRESS TRACKER
ISBN: 978-1-78783-533-7

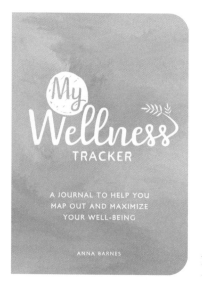

MY WELLNESS TRACKER
ISBN: 978-1-78783-638-9

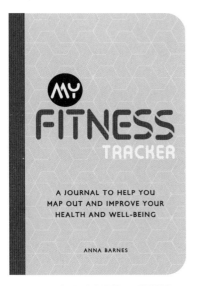

MY FITNESS TRACKER
ISBN: 978-1-80007-448-4

MY SLEEP TRACKER
ISBN: 978-1-78783-532-0

MY MOOD TRACKER
ISBN: 978-1-78783-328-9

Have you enjoyed this book?
If so, why not write a review on your
favourite website?

If you're interested in finding out more
about our books, find us on Facebook
at **Summersdale Publishers**, follow us
on Twitter at **@Summersdale** and on Instagram
at **@summersdalebooks** and get in touch.
We'd love to hear from you!

Thanks very much for buying this
Summersdale book.

www.summersdale.com

Image Credits